Amazing Dogs
Large Print Dot-to-Dot Book for Adults
Puzzles from 150 to 760 Dots

By Laura's Dot to Dot Therapy

<u>How To Use This Book</u>

Hi! We're so glad you're a lover of puzzles and dot connecting- we are too!

Connecting the dots in this book is simple- just relax and follow the numbers in consecutive order, drawing a straight line between each one. Dot 1 will connect to dot 2 and so on and so forth until there are no more dots to connect. There's always another dot and you'll always find it. Connect every dot to discover the beautiful images they create.

In case you get lost or can't find a dot, never stress- there's an answer key at the back of the book that will show you exactly where each dot connects to the next. If you want to color your images, we encourage you to do so! Feel free to try all different colors and coloring mediums for your images!

If you find any errors or omissions in this book, email us at Laurasdottodot@gmail.com and please let us know! We want you to have the best dot to dot experience!

Page 1

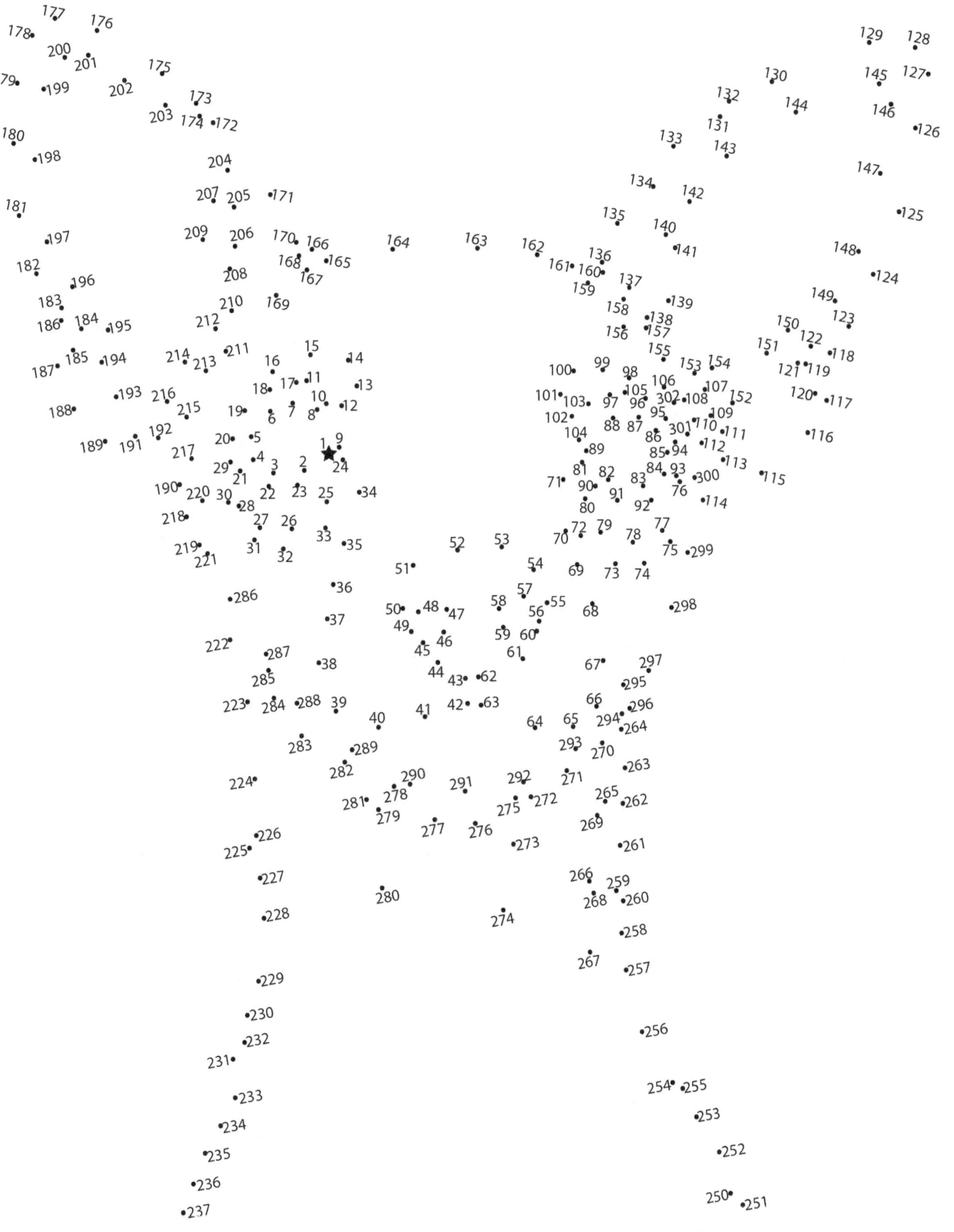

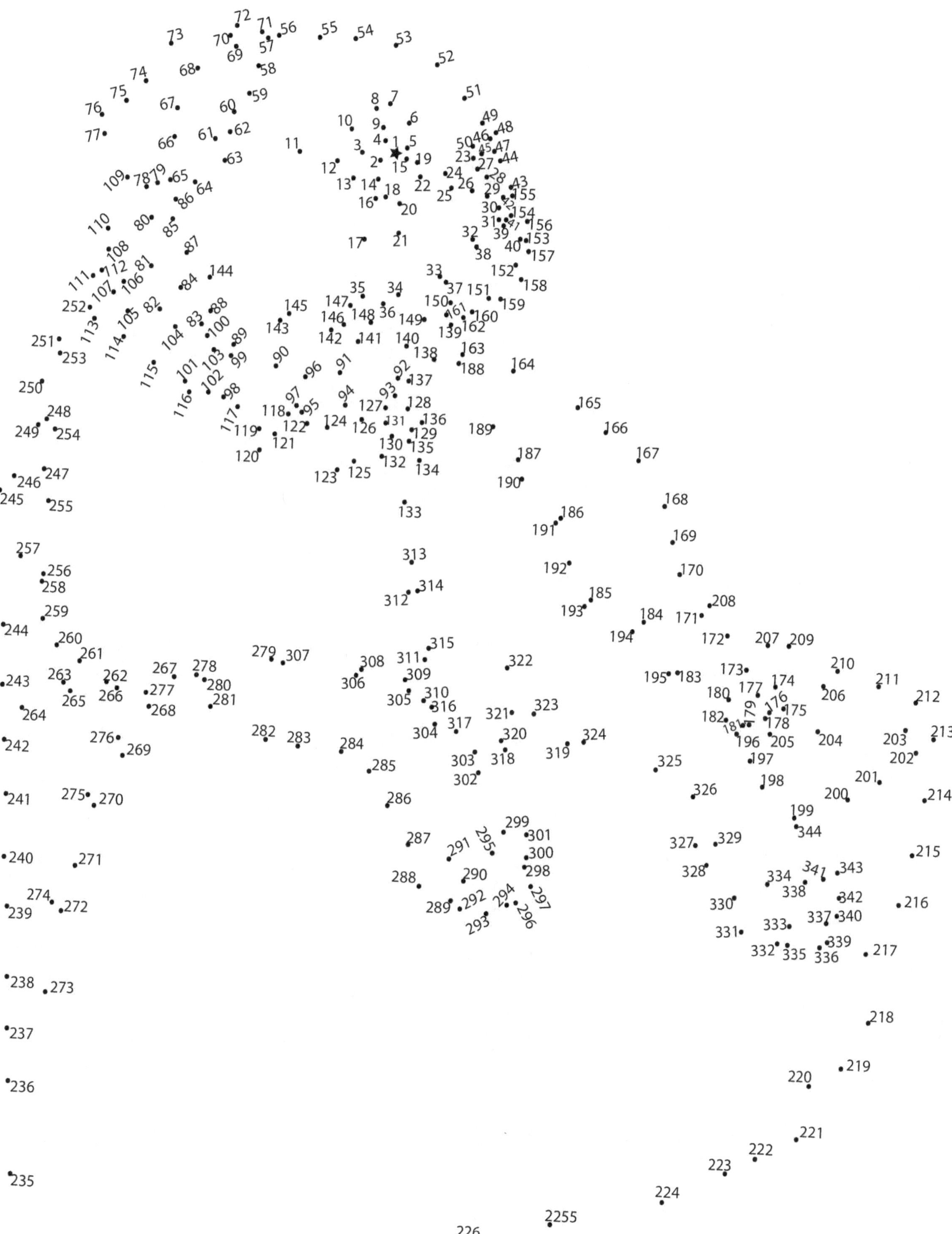

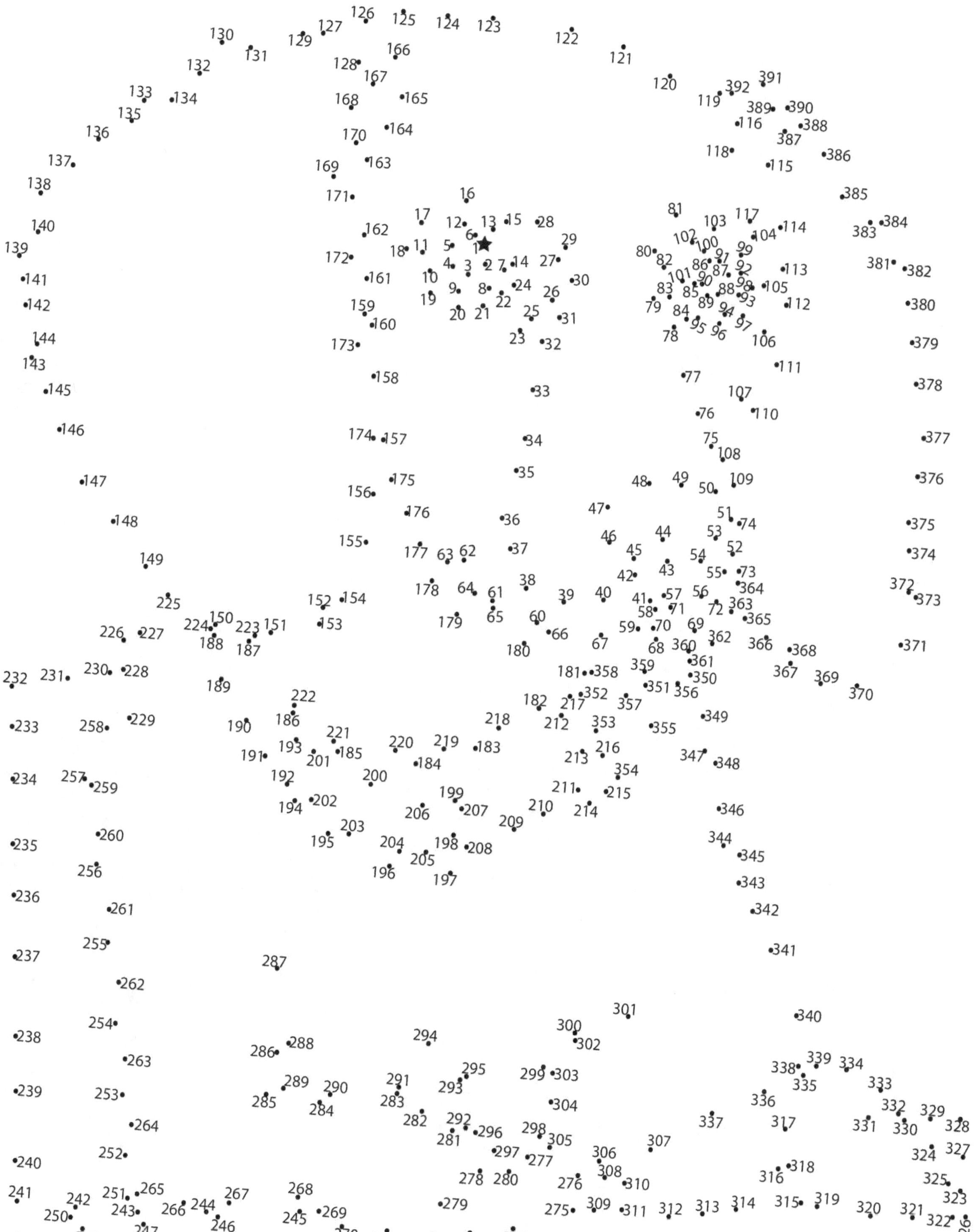

Page 5

Page 8

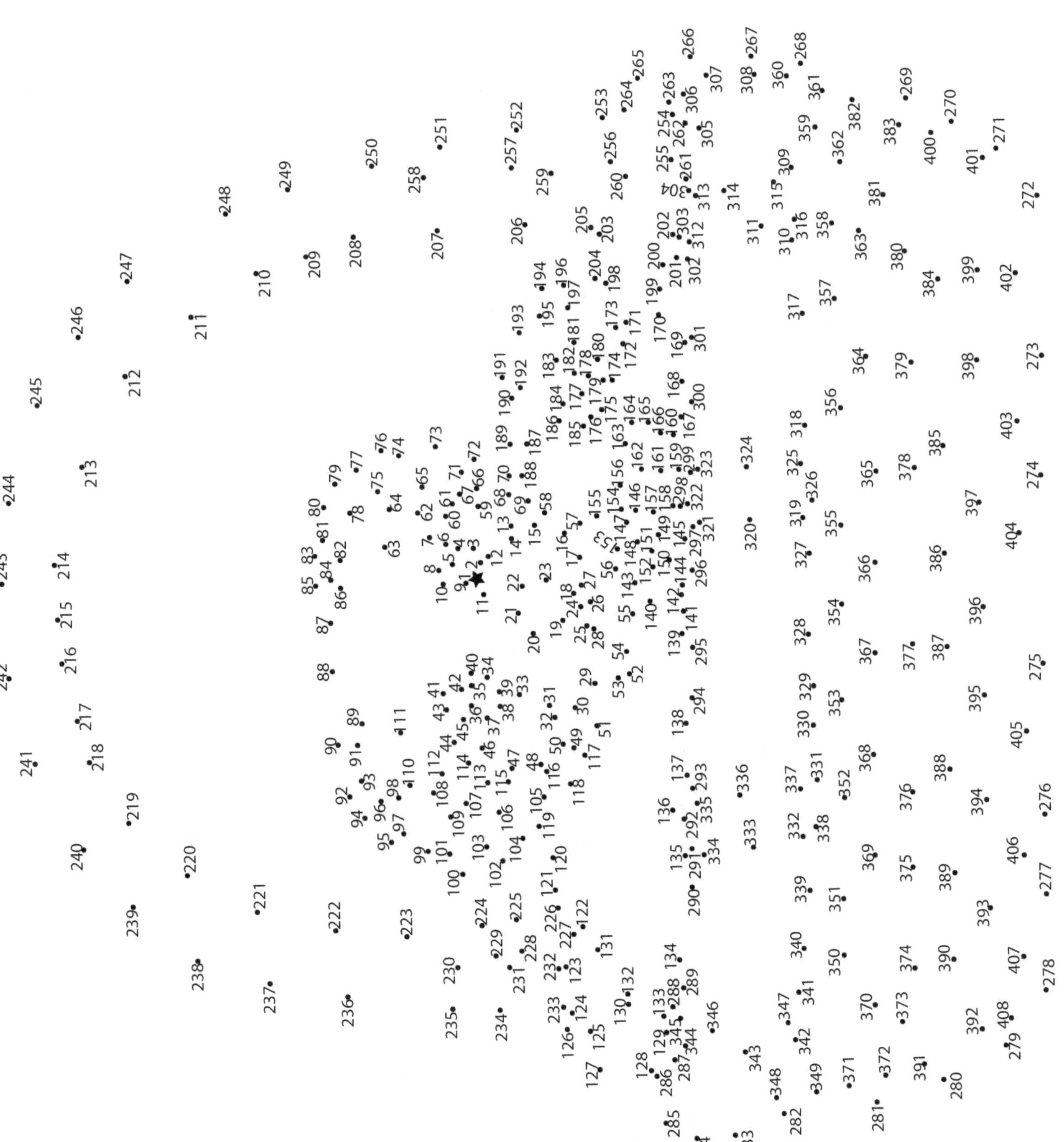

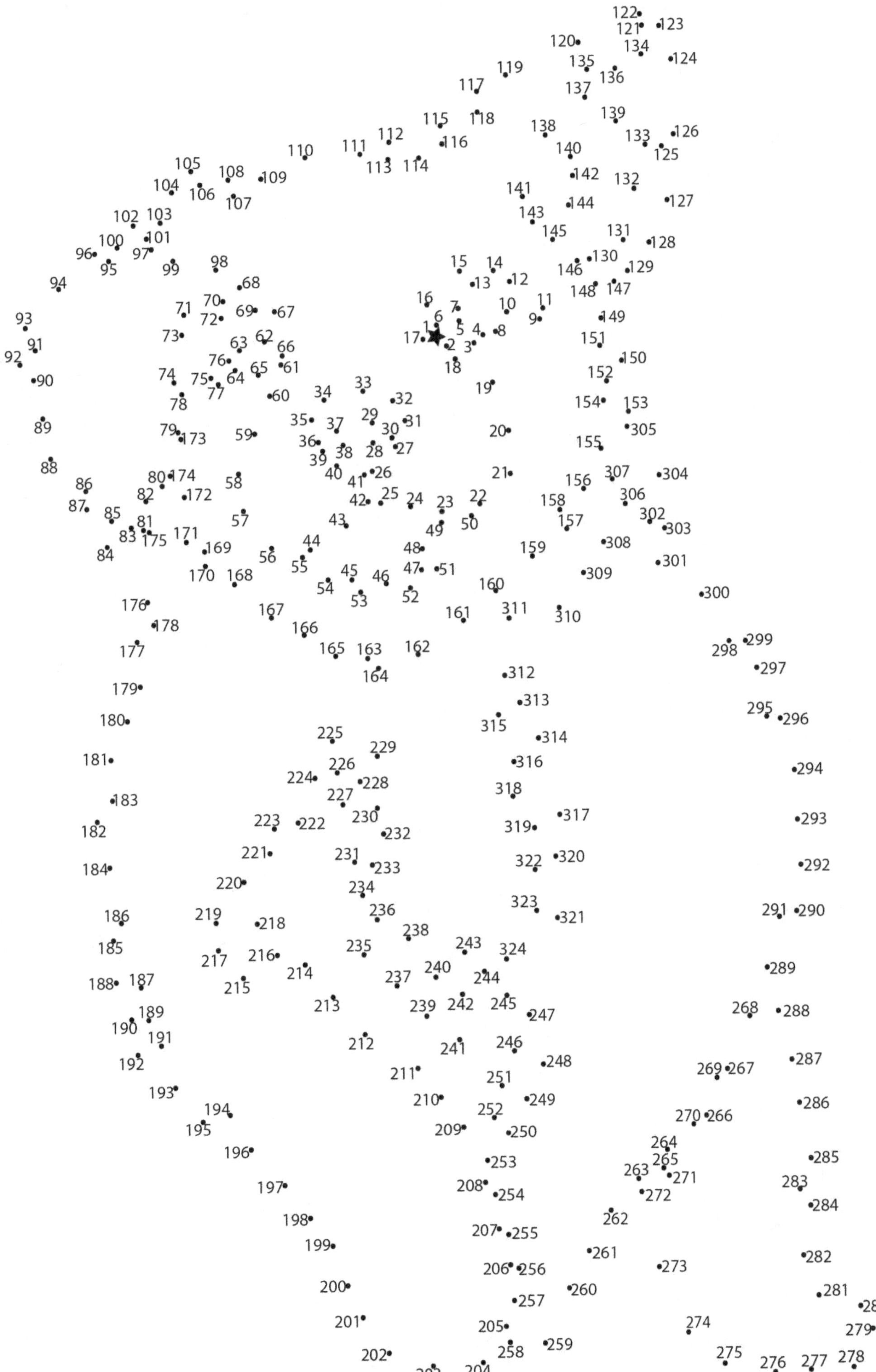

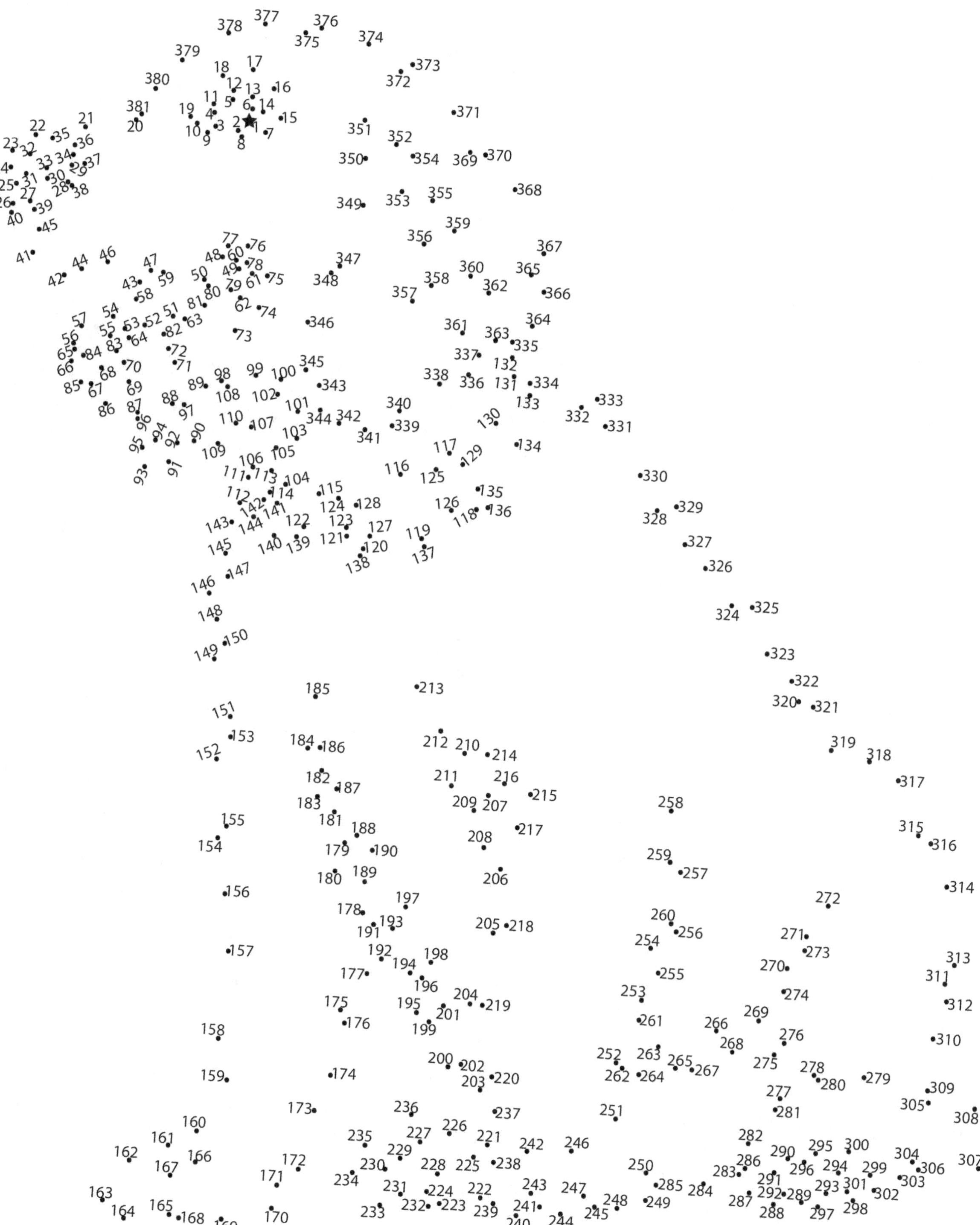

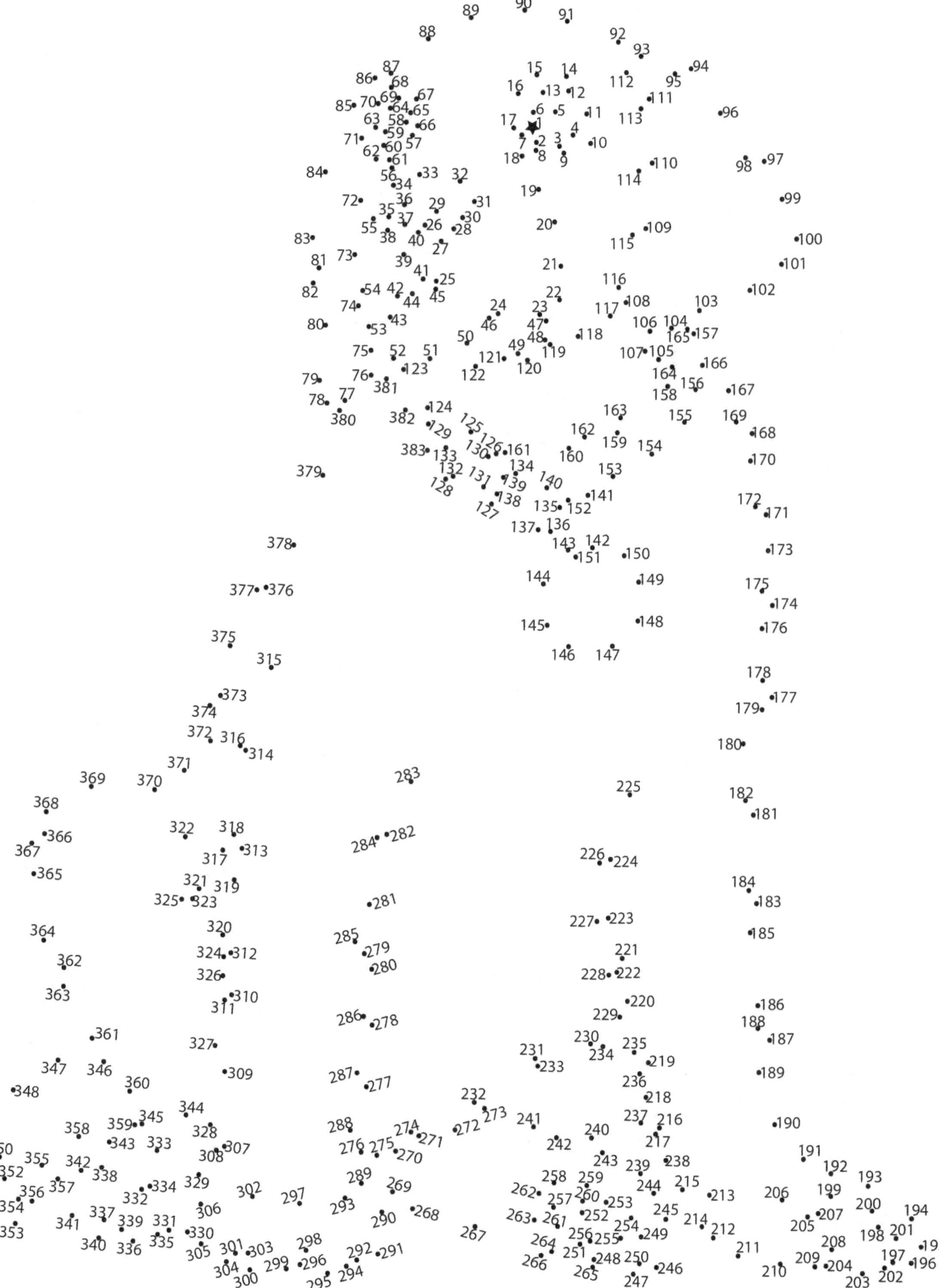

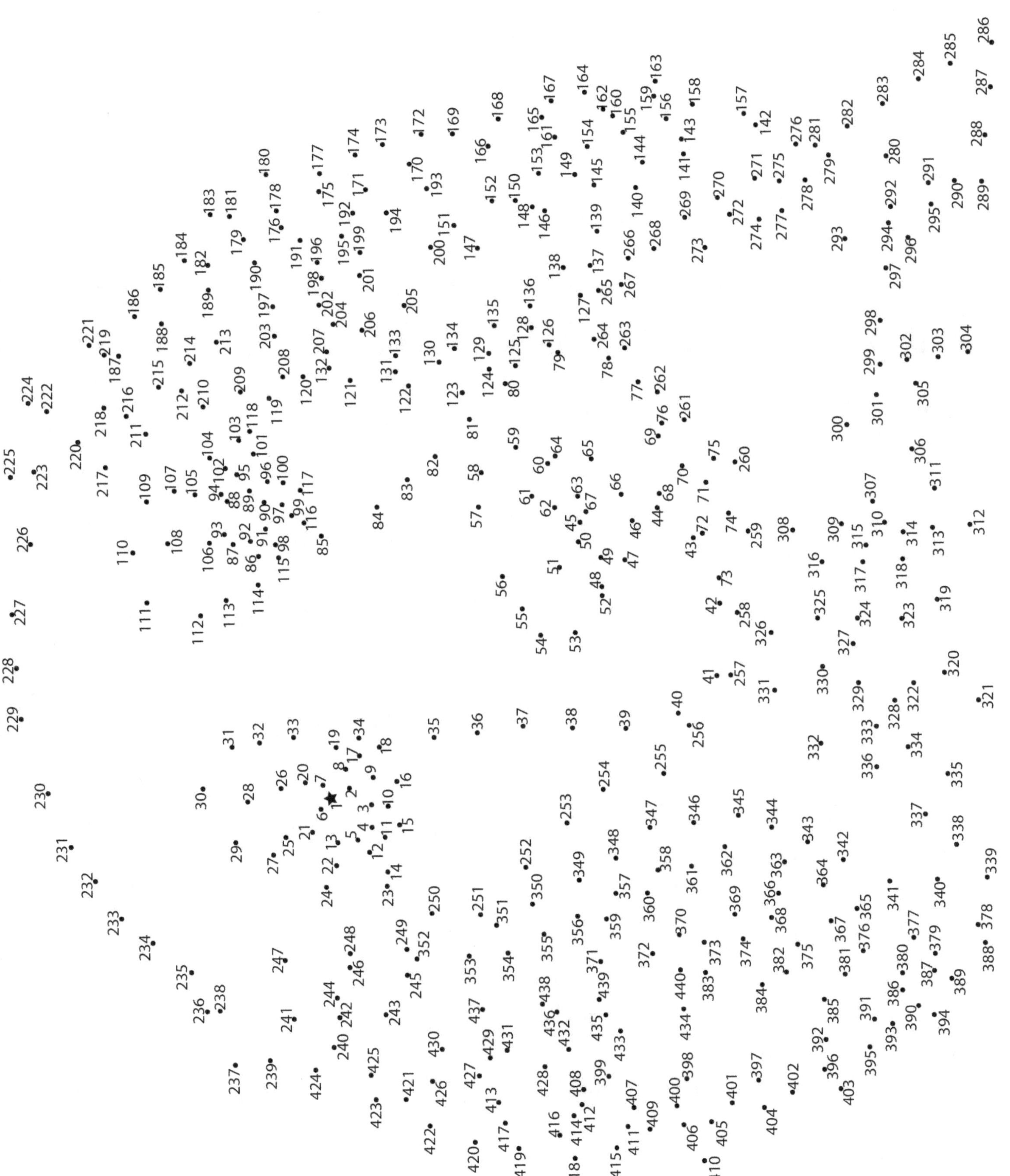

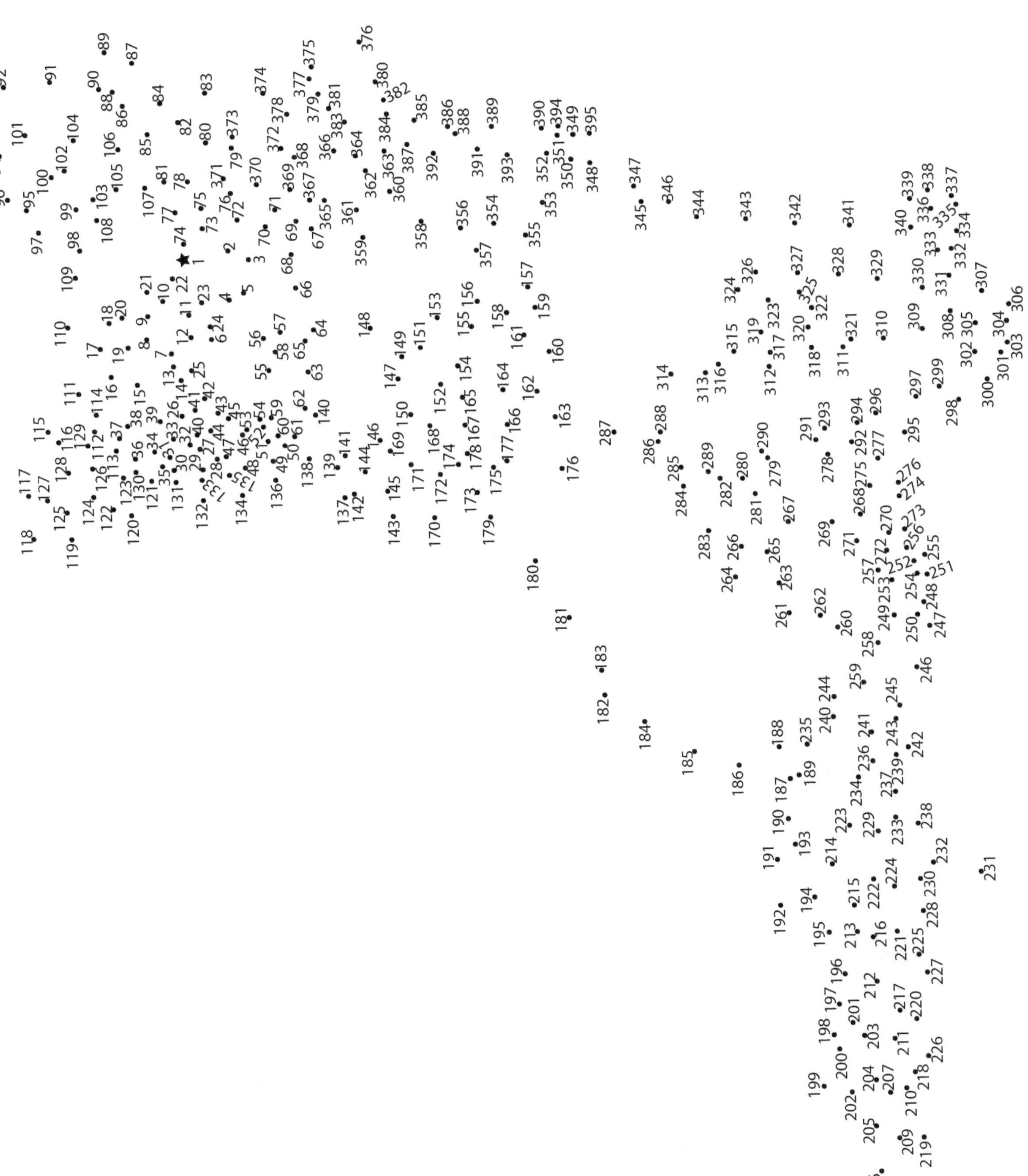

Enjoy bonus images from
some of our other fun
dot-to-dot books

Find all of our books on Amazon

Beautiful Flowers and Butterflies
Dot-to-Dot for Adults

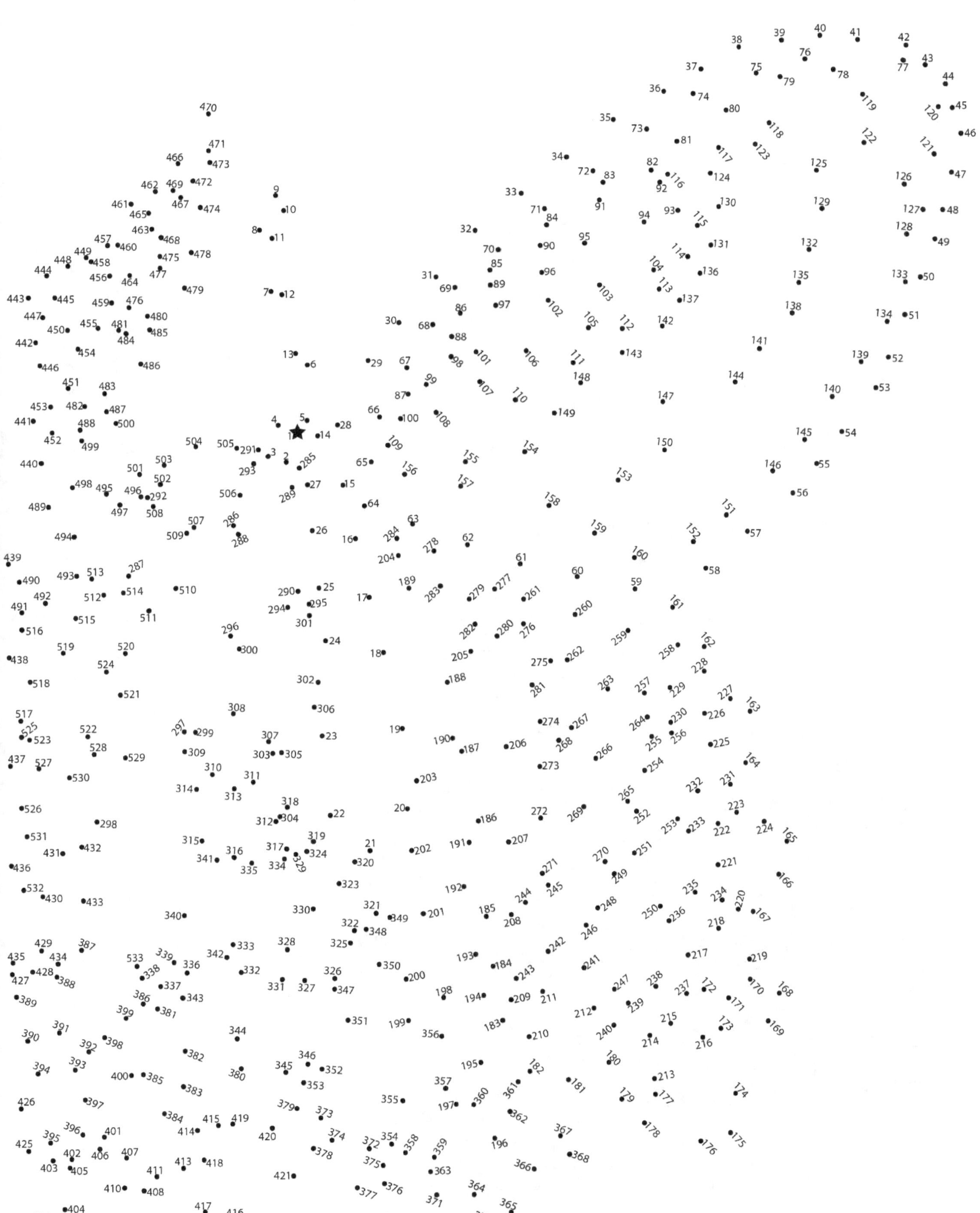

Cute Baby Animals Dot-to-Dot
Puzzles from 150 to 446 Dots

74 76 77
72 75 78 79 80 81
71 73 83 82
70 69 84
68 86 85
67 87
66
111 91 90 88
62 92 110 109 89
65 64 47 61 112 94 93 108
63 48 46 59
49 60 113 95
50 51 45 44 58 96 105 107 106
43 104
98 97
52 114
42
115 99
41 57 100 101 102 103
54 40 39 116 117
53 56 118
55 38
147 146 145 131
37
148 132 137 130 144
36 149 8 7 138 129
150 9 5 6 139 136
1 13 133 135 143 128
4 3 2 134 140 142
35 14 20 19 127
151 10 22 21 18 141 126
11 15 16 17 253 125 124
34 23 248 123
33 32 152 30 24 247 249 250 252 254
154 153 31 29 28 27 25 241 242 243 251 246 244 245 255 256
341 26 240 257
342 340 343 239 237 235 258
339 344 156 157 238 236 260
338 345 159 219 220 222 224 234 259
337 346 158 221 223 261
162 216 225 226 228 227 233 232 267 266 263 262 264 265 231
336 347 163 268
355 353 164 165 215 214 269
335 356 352 349 166 212 213 211 270 271
358 357 351 167 209 210 208 207 206 272
334 359 350 169 168 289 290 291 293 292 294 295 296 273
333 360 170 171 190 191 205 189 377 378 288 287 282 283 284 285 274
332 361 172 192 200 199 204 188 375 376 385 380 379 281 286 280 279 278 298 275
331 362 173 193 201 202 203 198 374 392 386 384 387 383 381 382 276 277 299 300 301
330 365 363 174 194 175 176 195 196 186 372 373 394 391 390 393 388 389 320 319 318 317 316 315 314 313 312 311 310 309 308 307 306 305 304 303 302
329 366 364 178 177 180 181 182 183 184 179 185 371 370 369 322 323 324 325 326 327 328 367 368

Answer Key

Follow along with the
page numbers from top left
to bottom right

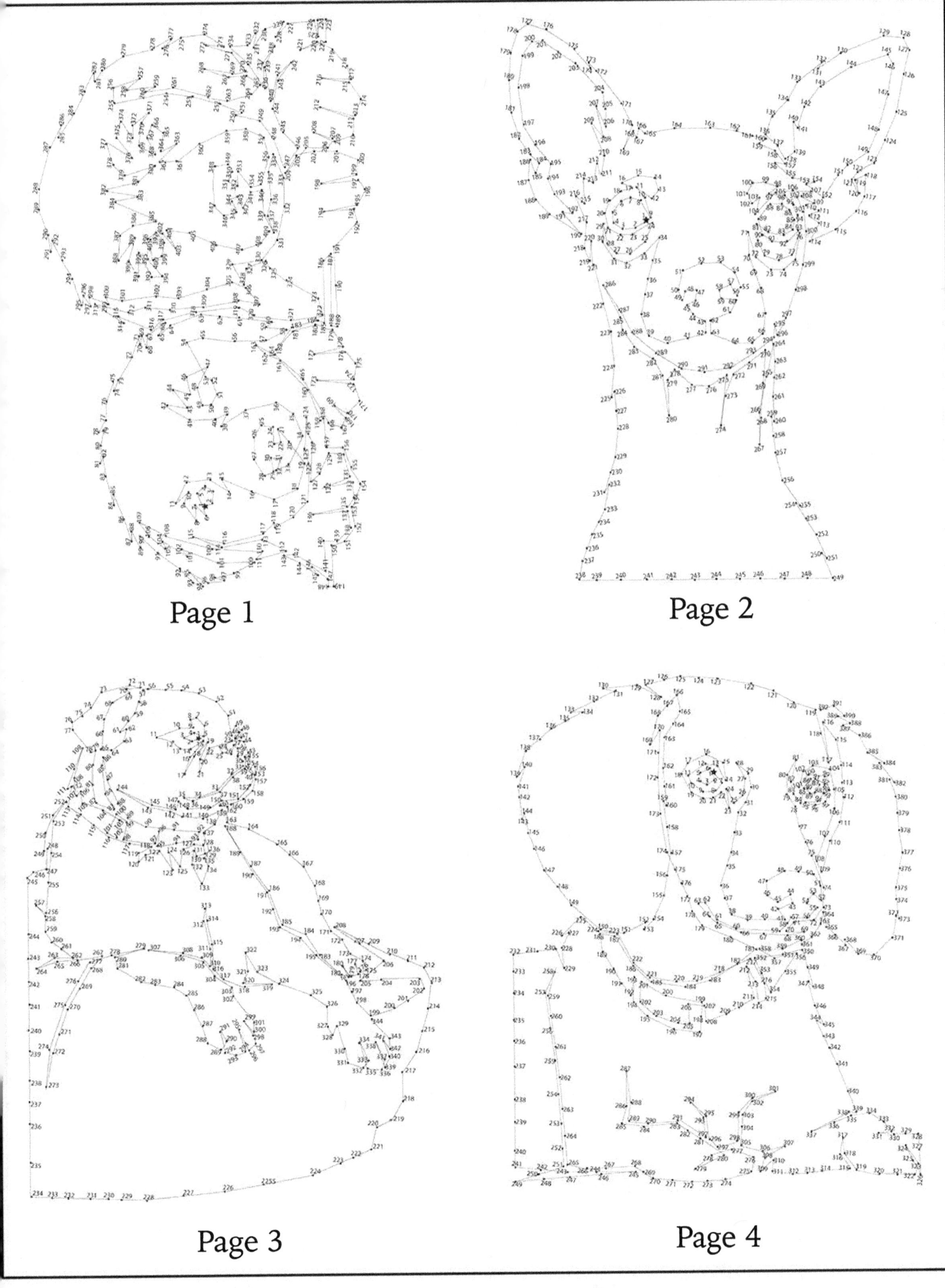

Page 1

Page 2

Page 3

Page 4

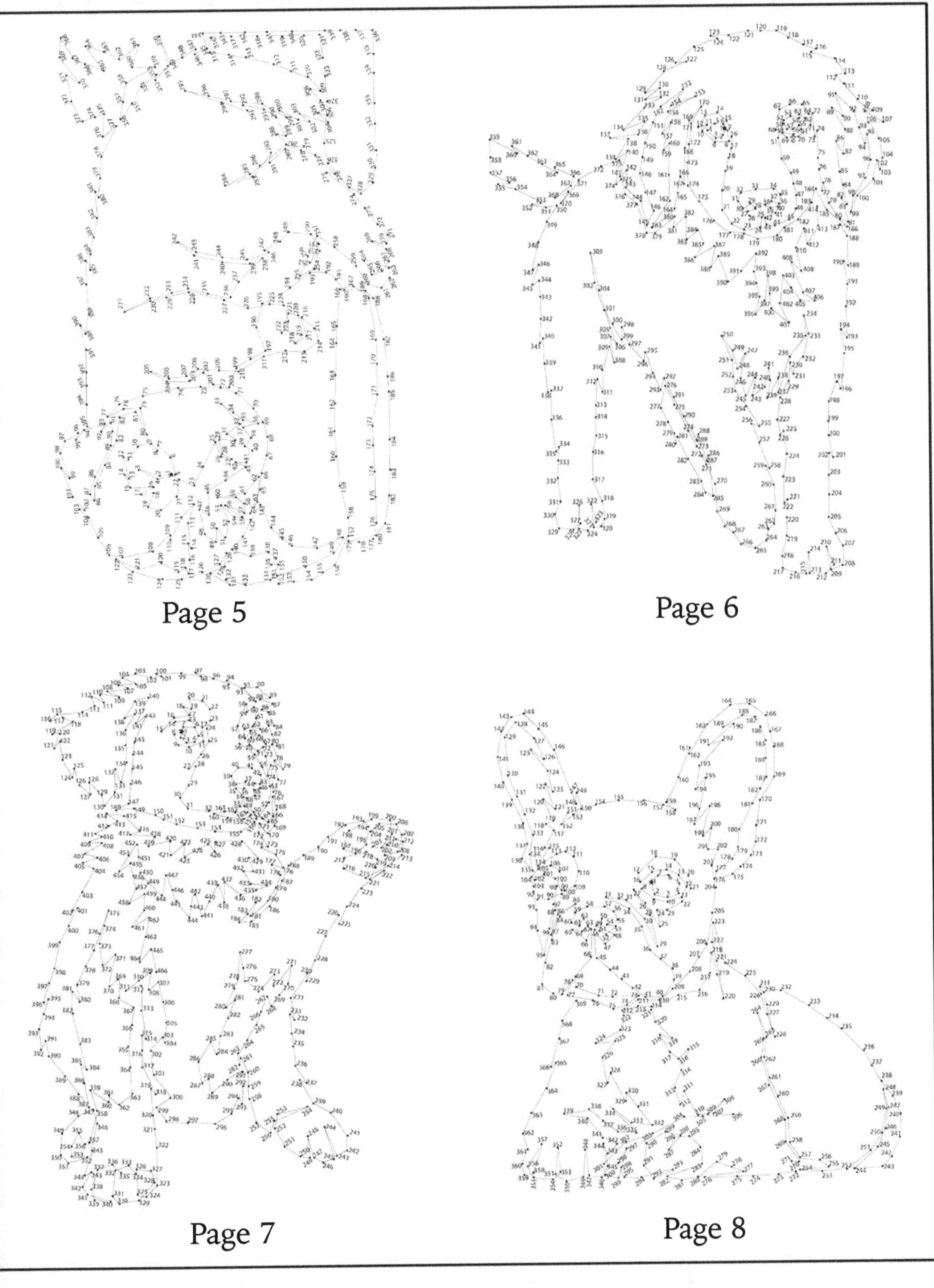

Page 5

Page 6

Page 7

Page 8

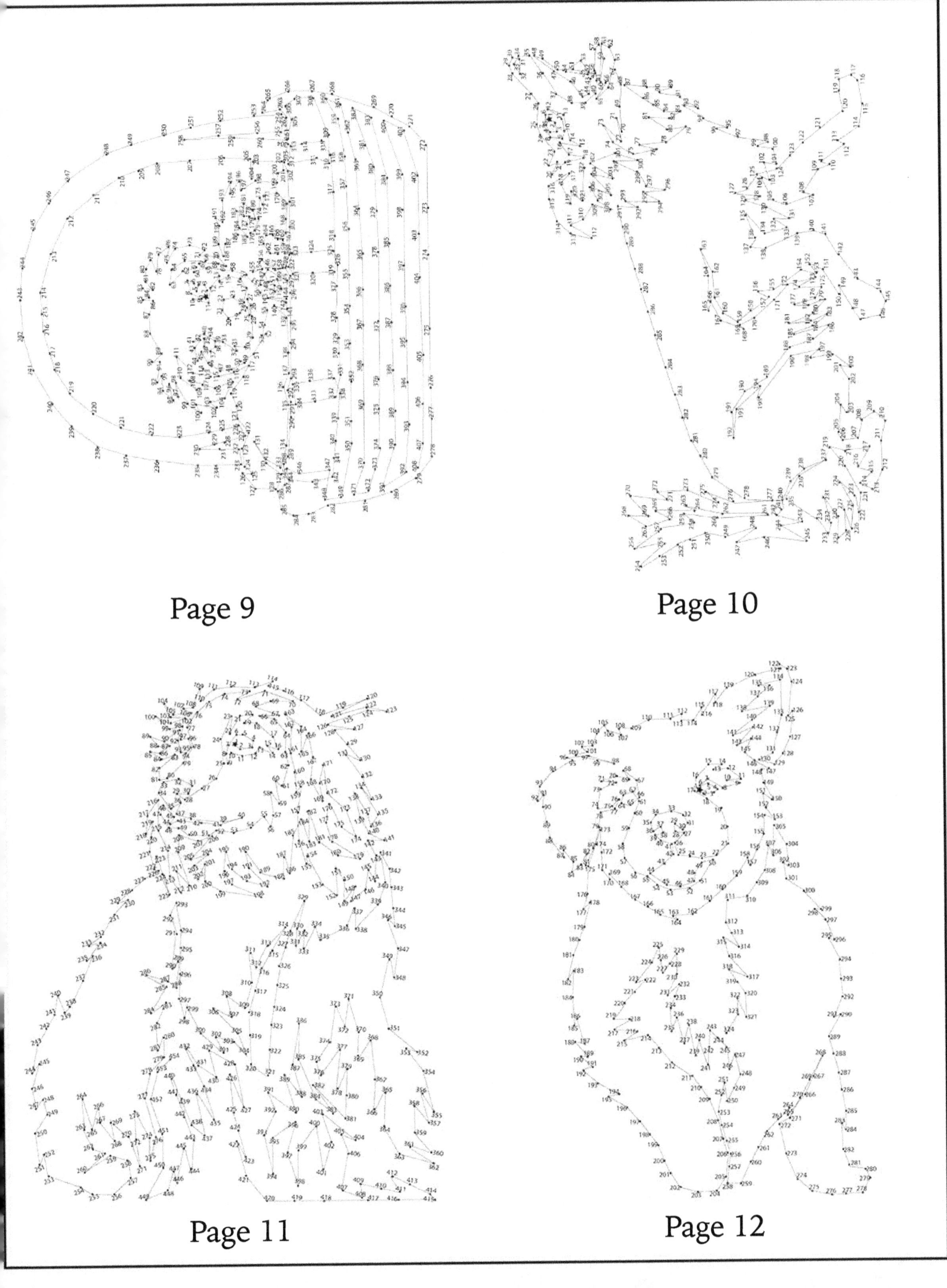

Page 9

Page 10

Page 11

Page 12

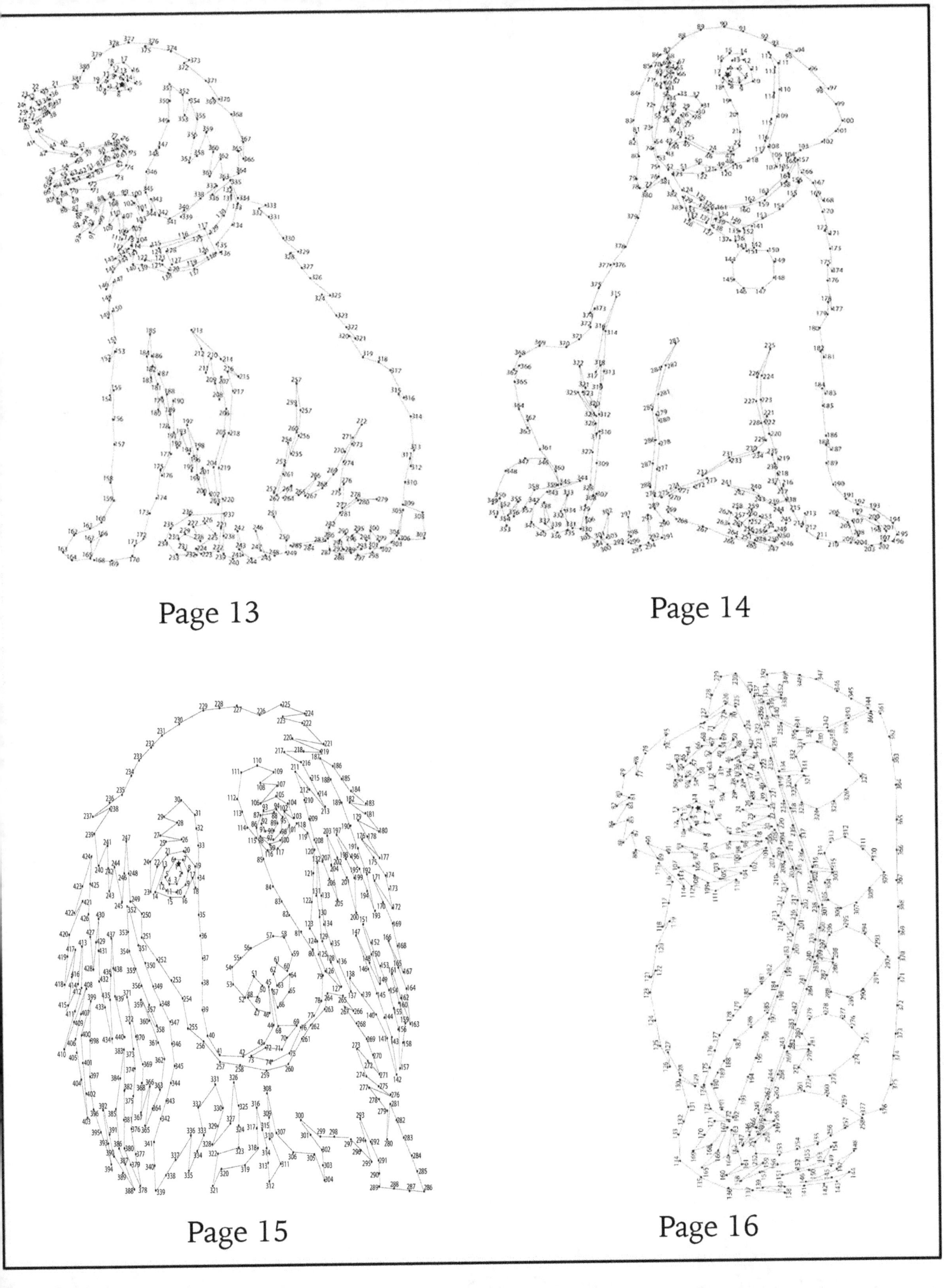

Page 13

Page 14

Page 15

Page 16

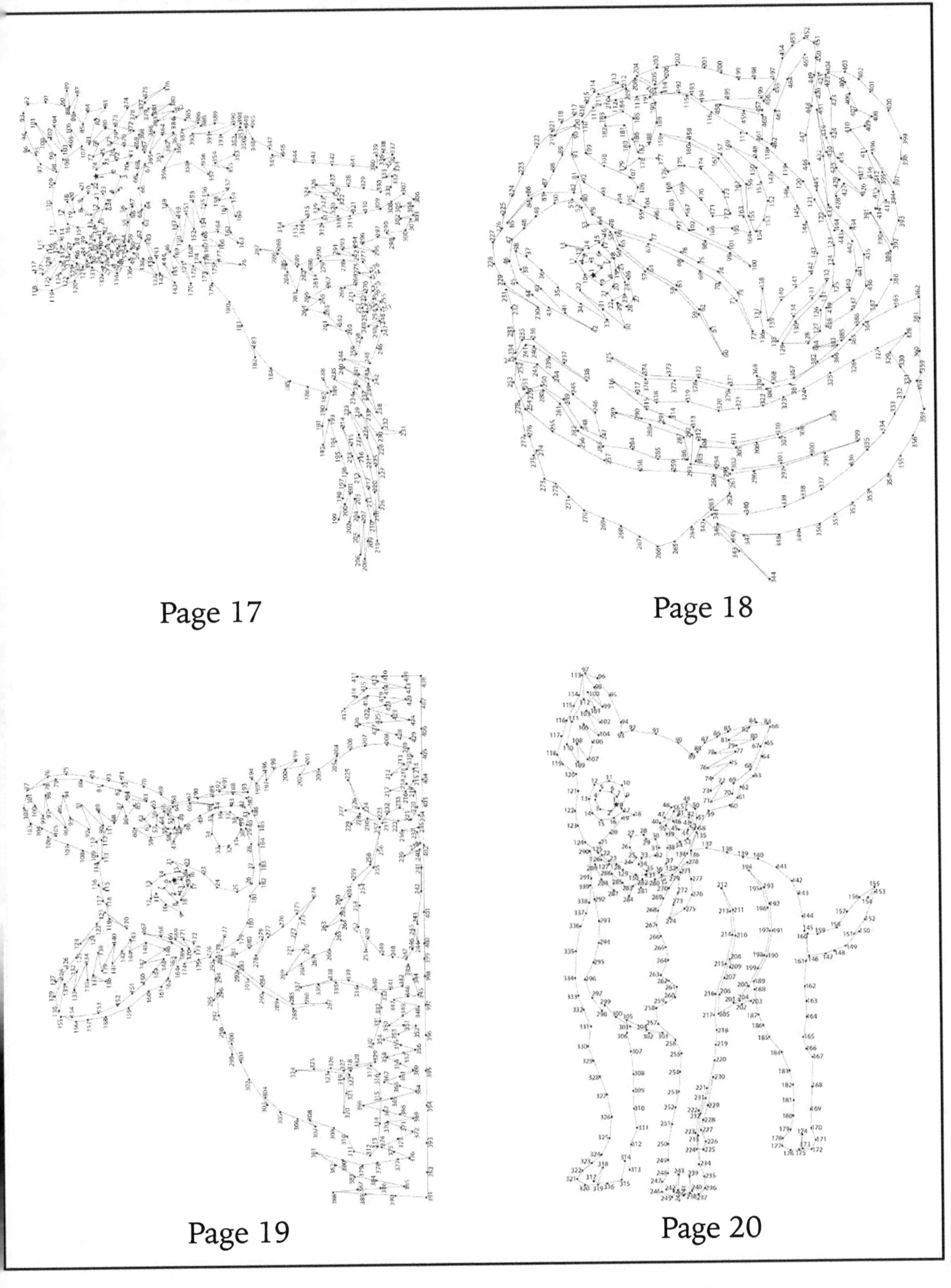

Page 17

Page 18

Page 19

Page 20

Please
Leave
Us
A Review
On Amazon

www.ingramcontent.com/pod-product-compliance
Lightning Source LLC
Chambersburg PA
CBHW081849250726
48659CB00008B/2672